Book

Preschool Skills
Alphabet

Illustrations by Maribel Suarez

An imprint of Sterling Children's Books

Published by Sterling Publishing Co., Inc.
387 Park Avenue South, New York, NY 10016
Text and illustrations © 2005 by Flash Kids
Distributed in Canada by Sterling Publishing
c/o Canadian Manda Group, 165 Dufferin Street
Toronto, Ontario, Canada M6K 3H6
Distributed in the United Kingdom by GMC Distribution Services
Castle Place, 166 High Street, Lewes, East Sussex, England BN7 1XU
Distributed in Australia by Capricorn Link (Australia) Pty. Ltd.
P.O. Box 704, Windsor, NSW 2756, Australia

Sterling ISBN 978-1-4114-3421-9

Manufactured in Canada

Lot #:
14 16 15 13
06/14

For information about custom editions, special sales, premium and
corporate purchases, please contact Sterling Special Sales
Department at 800-805-5489 or specialsales@sterlingpublishing.com.

Cover illustrations, design, and production by Mada Design, Inc.

Dear Parent,

Help your child build a solid foundation for reading and writing with this Preschool Skills workbook. Colorful illustrations and fun activities introduce the letters of the alphabet and help to strengthen your child's recognition of each letter. Your child will enjoy completing matching activities, finding hidden pictures, and learning to recognize uppercase and lowercase letters. Help your child make the most of this workbook with these tips:

- Provide a quiet, comfortable place for your child to complete this workbook. Go through each page with him or her slowly to ensure full comprehension of each activity.

- If your child answers a question incorrectly, explain why it is incorrect and allow your child to correct the mistake.

- Encourage your child to ask questions and have discussions about the things your child finds interesting in this book. You can also ask your child questions to keep him or her engaged in learning.

- Try to relate things found in this book to things your child encounters in everyday life. This will strengthen the connection between words and everyday objects.

- Most of all, enjoy this special time spent together! Reading to your child and helping him or her learn will build a strong bond between you both.

A Is for...

Apple

apple

Apples Are Awesome!

Circle the apples that show **A** or **a**.

B Is for...

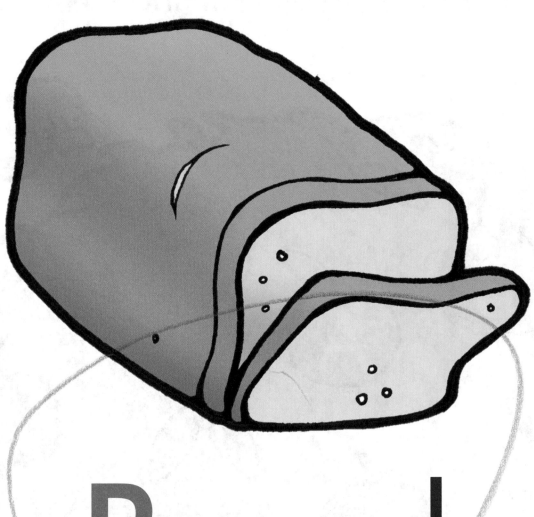

Bread

bread

Bring Me Bread!

Color the slices of bread
that show **B** or **b**.

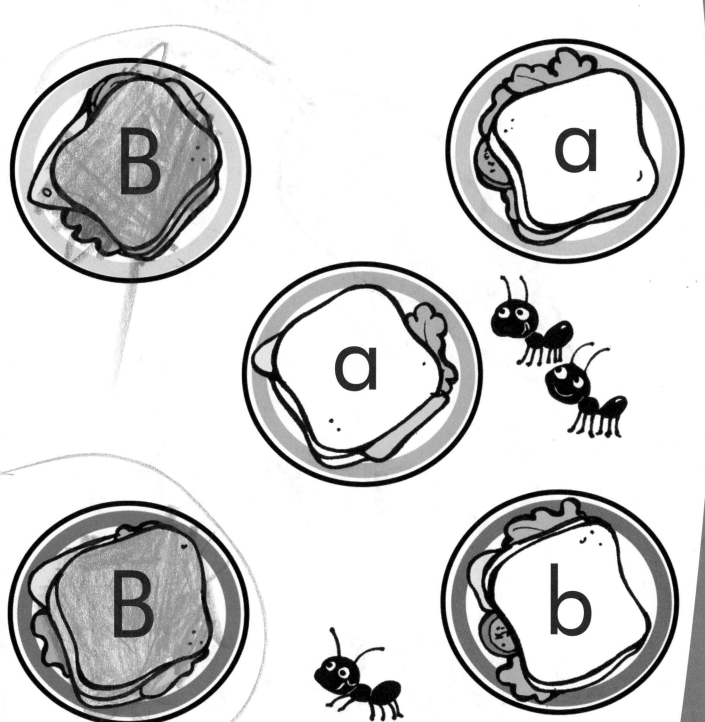

C Is for...

Carrot
carrot

Crunchy Carrots

Draw a line between
uppercase **C** and lowercase **c**.

D Is for...

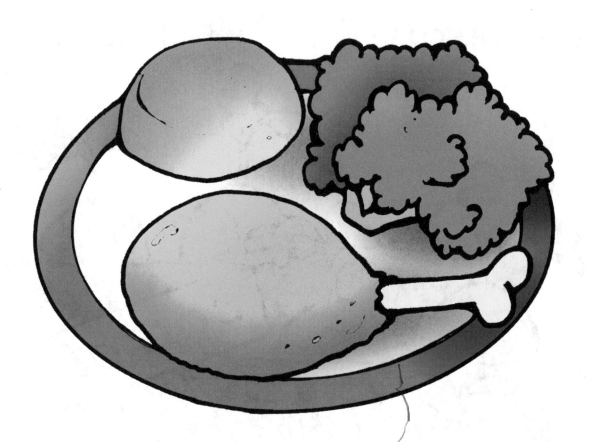

Dinner
dinner

Eating Eggs

Color the eggs that show **E** or **e**.

F Is for...

Fish
fish

Find the F Fish!

Circle the fish that show **F** or **f**.

G Is for...

Grapes
grapes

Grow, Grapes, Grow!

Draw a line between
uppercase **G** and lowercase **g**.

H Is for...

Hot dog
hot dog

Hungry for Hot Dogs!

Color the hot dogs that show **H** or **h**.

h c d H H h G H h

I Is for...

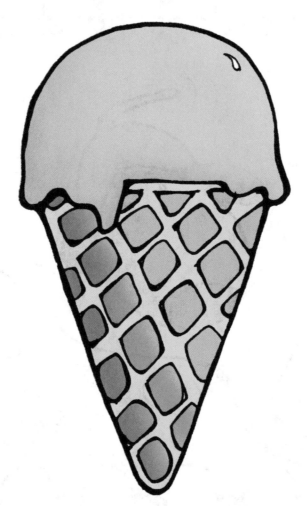

Ice cream
ice cream

I Love Ice Cream!

Color the ice cream sundaes
that show uppercase **I** and lowercase **i**.

J Is for...

Juice
juice

Jump for Juice

Circle the glasses that show **J** or **j**.
Color them the color of your
favorite juice.

K Is for...

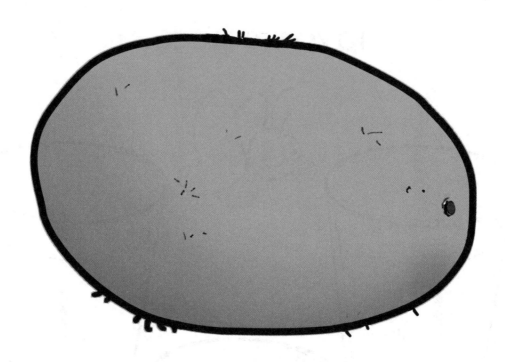

Kiwi
kiwi

Be Kind to Kiwis!

Circle the slices of kiwi
that show **K** or **k**.

L Is for...

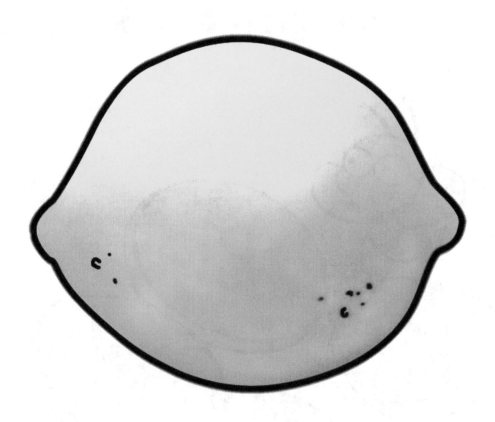

Lemon
lemon

Don't Lick a Lemon!

Draw a line between
uppercase **L** and lowercase **l**.

M Is for...

Milk
milk

Moo Cows!

Color the cows that show **M** or **m**.

N Is for...

Nuts
nuts

Nutty for Nuts!

Circle the nuts that show **N** or **n**.

O Is for...

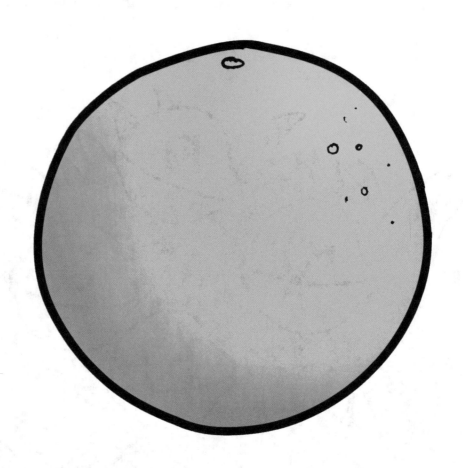

Orange
orange

Oodles of Oranges

Draw a line between
uppercase O and lowercase o.

P Is for...

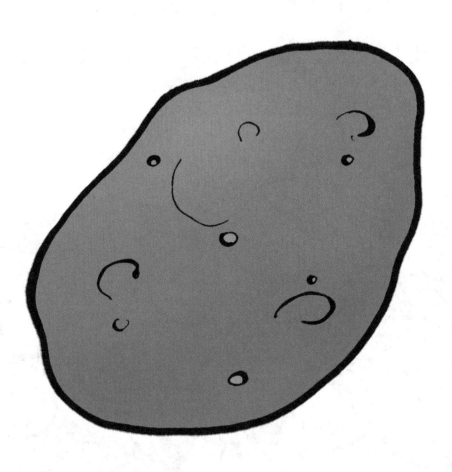

Potato

potato

Potato Party!

Circle the potatoes that show **P** or **p**.

Q Is for...

Quince
quince

A quince is a special fruit.

Quick Quinces

Color the quinces that show **Q** or **q**.

R Is for...

Rice
rice

Room for Rice

Circle the bowls of rice that show **R** or **r**.

S Is for...

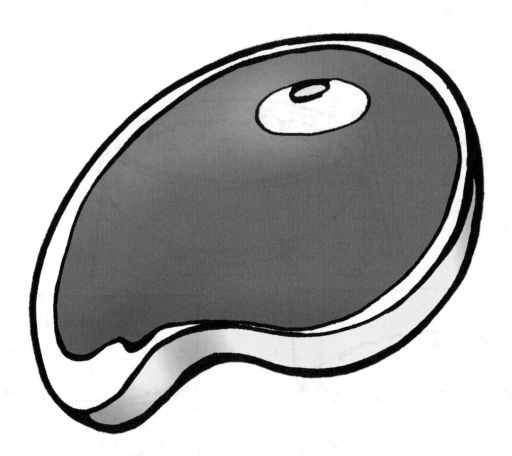

Steak
steak

Sizzling Steaks!

Color the steaks that show **S** or **s**.

T Is for...

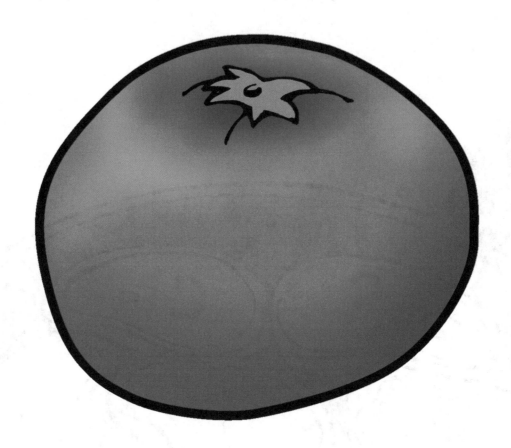

Tomato
tomato

Tasty Tomatoes

Draw a line between
uppercase **T** and lowercase **t**.

U Is for...

Utensils
utensils

Use Your Utensils!

Circle the utensils that show **U** or **u**.

V Is for...

Vegetables
vegetables

Very Good Vegetables!

Circle the vegetables that show **V** or **v**.

W Is for...

Watermelon
watermelon

Watermelons Are Wonderful!

Draw a line between
uppercase **W** and lowercase **w**.

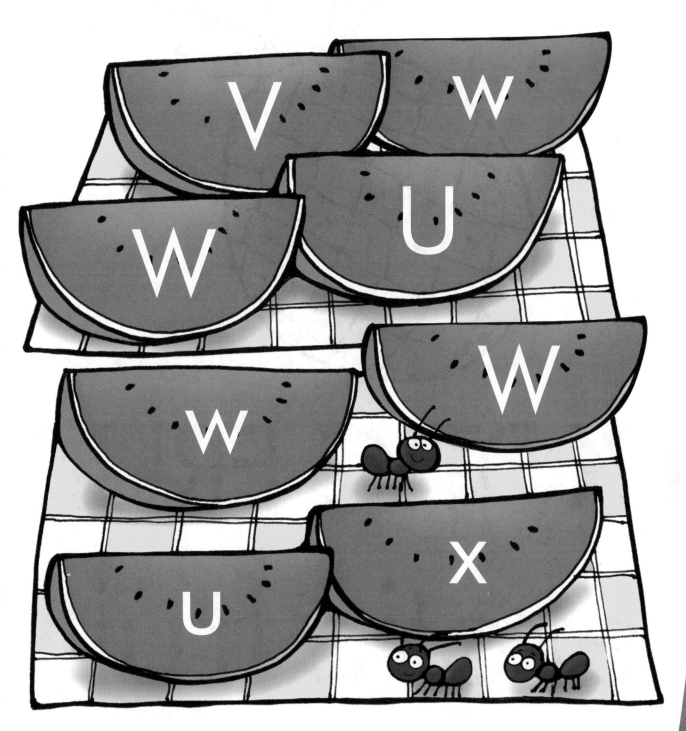

X Is for...

EXOTIC FRUIT
exotic fruit

Exotic Fruit Are Extra Special!

Color the exotic fruit that show **X** or **x**.

Y Is for...

Yogurt
yogurt

Yogurt Is Yummy!

Draw a line between
uppercase **Y** and lowercase **y**.

Z Is for...

Zucchini
zucchini

Zucchini Zone

Color the zucchinis that show **Z** or **z**.

The Alphabet

Trace the alphabet.

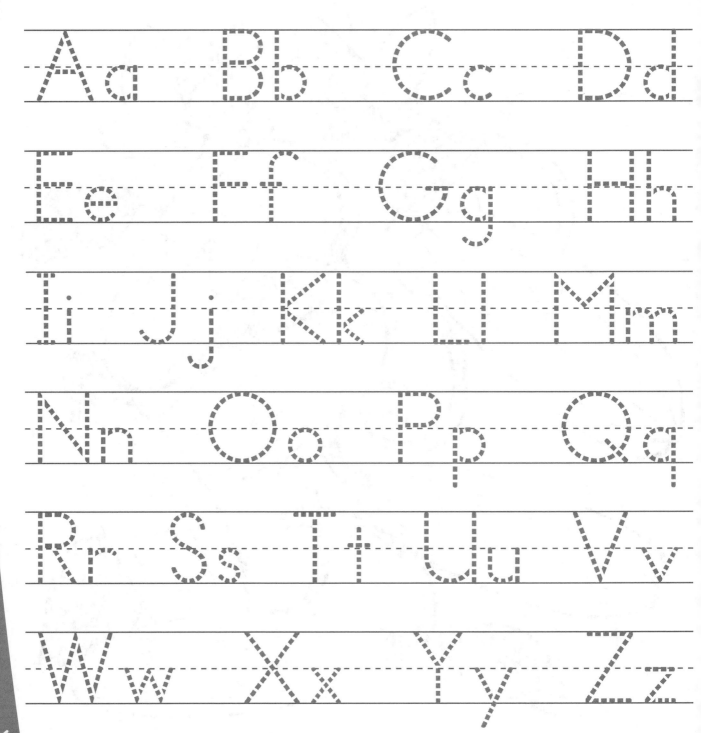

Beginning Letters

Color the foods that begin with **c**.

chicken

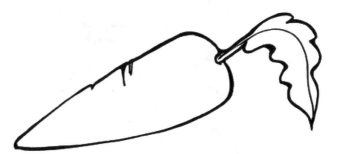

carrot

corn

tomato

cookie

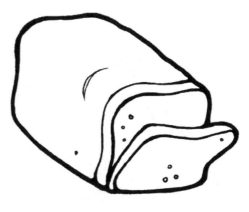

bread

Ending Letters

Color the foods that end with **s**.

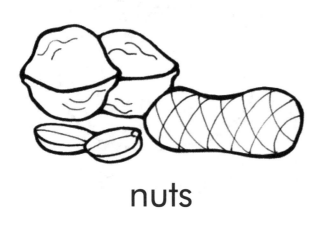

grapes

bananas

nuts

yogurt

pizza

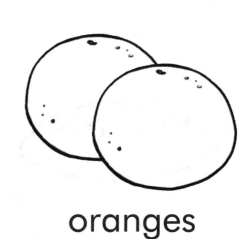

oranges

Matching Letters

Draw a line to match each uppercase letter to its lowercase letter.

More Matching Letters

Draw a line to match each lowercase letter to its uppercase letter.

Time for Dessert!

Find the hidden picture.
Color the spaces that show **I** or **i**.

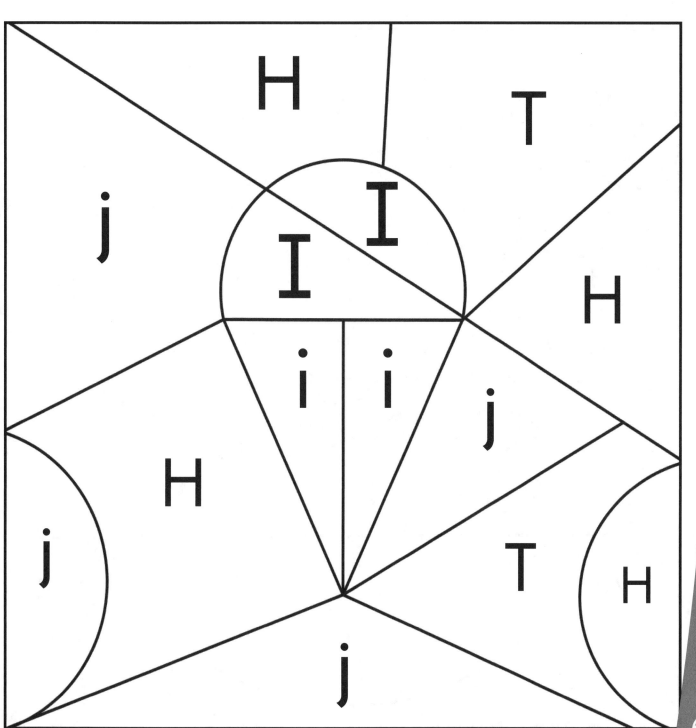

And Seconds!

Find the hidden picture. Color the spaces that show **B** or **b**.

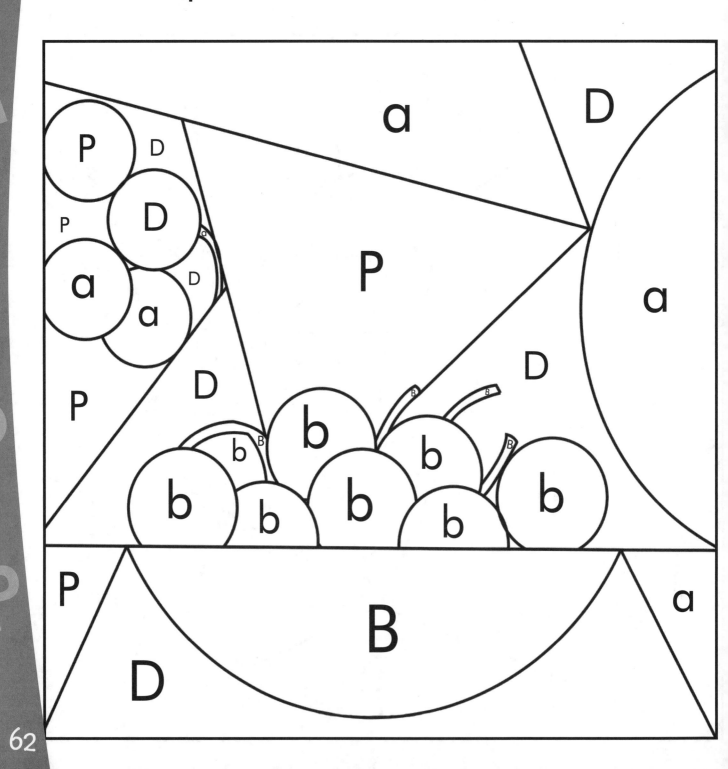

And Thirds!

Find the hidden picture.
Color the spaces that show **A** or **a**.

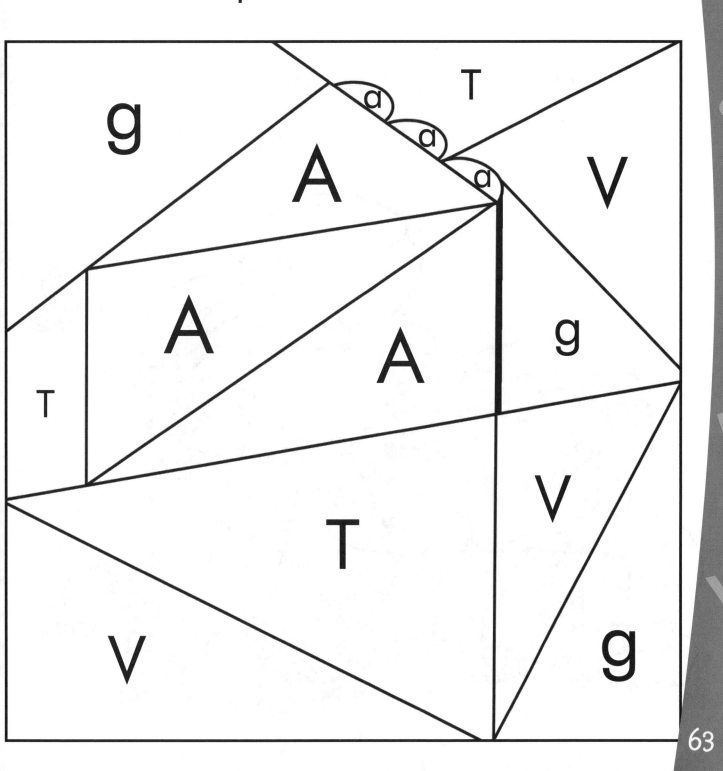

_____,
(Name)

you did a great job learning
the letters of the alphabet!